Quack This Way

Quack
This
Way

David Foster Wallace &
Bryan A. Garner Talk
Language and Writing

February 3, 2006
Hilton Checkers Hotel
Los Angeles, California

David Foster Wallace (1962–2008) was probably the greatest writer of his generation. He wrote the acclaimed novels *Infinite Jest* and *The Broom of the System*, as well as the story collections *Oblivion, Brief Interviews with Hideous Men,* and *Girl with Curious Hair.* His nonfiction includes the essay collections *Consider the Lobster* and *A Supposedly Fun Thing I'll Never Do Again,* together with the full-length *Everything and More* and the posthumously published commencement speech *This Is Water.* He committed suicide in September 2008.

Bryan A. Garner (b. 1958), author and lexicographer, has written more than 20 books on English usage, legal writing, advocacy, business writing, and more, including *Garner's Dictionary of Legal Usage, Garner's Modern American Usage,* and *Reading Law: The Interpretation of Legal Texts* (with Justice Antonin Scalia). Garner is the editor in chief of *Black's Law Dictionary* and Distinguished Research Professor of Law at Southern Methodist University. He founded LawProse, Inc., a Dallas-based training and consulting firm, in 1990.

ROSEPEN

RosePen Books, Dallas, Texas 75254
©2013 by Bryan A. Garner
All rights reserved. Published 2013.
Printed in the United States of America.

ISBN-13: 978-0-991-11811-3

Cover illustrations by L.W. Montgomery, Boise, Idaho.

Contents

Introduction 1
The interview 23
    The reader cannot read your mind 25
    Crummy, turgid, verbose, abstruse,
        abstract, solecism-ridden prose 43
    The trunk cable into the linguistic heart 67
    Never let the reader forget what
        the stakes are here 76
    You need to quack this way 98
Index 125

Introduction

I t must have been late 1999 when my secretary, Andrea, excitedly proclaimed that David Foster Wallace had just called the office and spoken to her.

"Who?" I said.

"David Foster Wallace!"

"Who's he?"

She explained that he was a major, major writer—the author of *Infinite Jest*. I knew the book.

"He's writing something about you," she gushed.

"Why didn't you put me on the phone with him?"

"I offered," Andrea said, "but he refused. He said he didn't want to speak with you directly. He just wanted some basic information about you. Apparently he's reviewing your usage book."

I went on with my day and put it mostly out of my mind. Apparently I wrote him a note in March 2000—a note I no longer have.

Then, a few weeks later, I received a massive manuscript from Bloomington, Illinois. It was David's manuscript of "Tense Present." The cover letter may have been the first of David's writing I'd ever read. It was self-effacing, apologetic, and endearing. He kept insisting that I shouldn't feel obliged to read the whole review, even though he'd worked "a whole bloody two months" on it. He wrote: "I usually hate it when people send me their work to read unsolicited, so I'm bending way over backward here to assure you that I enclose it with no expectations and nothing but good wishes."

But of course I did read it, and it was enormously impressive.

It took awhile for "Tense Present" to get published. Originally commissioned by *The New Republic*, it was rejected by the editors there as unwieldy. Then it spent some time (as I was later to learn) at *The New York Review of Books*. In the end, it appeared as the cover article of *Harper's*— in April 2001. The *Harper's* editors cut the piece in half but showed real creativity in printing it on a bluish paper in the middle of the magazine, as if it were a special section produced separately. They managed to include 52 of the 124 footnotes in his piece—which ended up, in the full version published in *Consider the Lobster* (2005), more than twice as long. That version is called "Authority and American Usage."

The review is a long, laudatory piece. It changed my literary life in ways that a book review rarely can.

Things began happening that had never happened before. For example, in May 2001, a month after the review appeared, I happened to be in Cambridge, Massachusetts, at the Harvard Co-Op—the university's main bookshop. I ducked into the shop because I had 15 minutes to kill before a dinner with a friend. With two linguistic books tucked under my arm, I went to the checkout line and stood behind a man I immediately recognized as Pulitzer prize-winner Anthony Lewis. I had met him the year before at a dinner for the American Law Institute, and I considered whether to reintroduce myself. I decided not to but instead to respect his privacy and let him get on with his afternoon. He seemed mildly fretful about getting through the checkout line, and I figured he might be writing a *New York Times* editorial in his head, working against a tight deadline. Finally he got to the front of the line and handed the cashier his one book for purchase.

It was my *Dictionary of Modern American Usage* (as it was then called), with its distinctive red cover. So I approached him after all, slightly interrupting his transaction, and introduced myself. "Bryan! I've just been reading the Wallace review in *Harper's,* and I hastened over here to get the book before finishing the review."

We had a good chat.

Now what are the chances of that? I'd had a few minutes to spare before meeting with a friend. I'd gone into the Harvard Co-Op to take a whirlwind scan of the reference, linguistics, and law sections; and I'd rushed to the checkout line at the precise moment when I'd be in line behind Anthony Lewis, who was buying my book.

Another remarkable thing about that afternoon: the Co-Op had stocked about 20 copies of my usage book, piling them on the floor in the reference section as well as displaying them prominently on the shelves. Never before had I seen more than two copies of one of my books in a bookstore—apart from *Black's Law Dictionary* in law-school bookstores.

This was all new to me.

A few weeks before, I had received a call from a Boston public-radio station asking whether I'd participate in a joint interview with David Foster Wallace. He had requested my participation. I agreed, of course. It was a fascinating interview, and it was the first time we spoke to each other. (We still didn't meet, though: we were both calling into the station.) He called me "Mr. Garner" throughout—as he would for many months after. The interview can still be heard at http://theconnection.wbur.org/2001/03/30/english-language-usage.

Soon we were corresponding intermittently. He wanted to see one of my legal-writing seminars in Chicago. I said I'd be delighted, if we could arrange it.

Then, in April 2002, the State Farm Insurance Company in Bloomington, Illinois, asked me to present one of my private seminars to about 100 of its lawyers. I wrote to David to ask whether he'd like to have dinner the night before. "Yes!" came the answer.

He wanted to attend the seminar as well. This, I thought at the time, might be a problem. My client was paying a significant fee for an in-house seminar. They were insurance-company lawyers. Stalwart conservatives—if true to the stereotype. I'd be asking to have a bandana-wearing novelist and essayist attend—somebody I'd not yet seen face to face. Although I already trusted David, I ended up not trusting myself: I might not teach in quite the same way if he were in the audience. I might not do as well for the State Farm lawyers. And I wouldn't want to extract a pledge from him that he couldn't write about the event. After all, his sardonic wit might prompt him to write about my client as he'd already written about the Maine Lobster Festival or the adult-film-awards festival.

I told him he shouldn't attend. He understood. We'd settle on a public seminar someday soon.

That almost happened in Chicago in 2002 and again in Los Angeles in 2006 or 2007. But someday never came.

In the lead-up to our dinner in Bloomington, which occurred on May 28, 2002, David's outrageous humor started to show. In an e-mail (Feb. 18), he said his mother would like to be there. "She won't feel you up or anything," he assured me, "she's just a fan."

I said yes, she could come.

Then he followed up by writing (Feb. 22): "You may get your tie ripped off like the Beatles c. 1965, I'm warning you right now." He was joking, I knew. Flagrantly.

Then another message came: David's father, James, would like to attend just to ensure that nothing untoward might happen. Would that be all right?

Of course, I said.

When the day arrived, I took a cab from the Bloomington airport to two used-book stores (as is my habit), bought two boxes of books (again, my habit), and headed to the hotel where David was to pick me up. He was right on time.

"David?" I asked with outstretched hand.

"Glad to meet you, Bryan." His handshake was not firm, and he mostly averted his eyes. He was shy.

He led me to his car and we drove to the restaurant, Biaggi's, on Veterans Parkway in Bloomington. He assured me that he'd been exaggerating about his mother and said that all would be okay with his father present. After a wrong turn or two—he was a nervous driver—we arrived at the restaurant.

The Hilton Checkers Hotel in Los Angeles (site of the interview)

His parents were already there, and we all felt comfortable after introductions. I told them about my rare-book finds and asked whether David collected books.

"I don't *collect*, really, but I have plenty."

We talked of books, writing, grammar, his mother's grammar book, the possibility that David might cowrite a book with his mother, James's teaching of philosophy at Urbana-Champaign, my own teaching routine, and many other things.

David had ordered a Coke—in a can, he specified, not in a glass. He took a few sips, I noticed, and then stopped sipping when putting the Coke can to his mouth. He was subtly spitting into it. He had what looked to be snuff in his lower lip, and he was spitting into a Coke can that was not quite full. This was between courses—after appetizers. Having grown up in the Texas Panhandle, I was well familiar with snuff, but never at the table between courses.

When David left to go to the restroom, I couldn't help asking his parents: "Is David drinking that Coke?"

"No," his mother said. "He drinks just enough to make room for his spit. He dips snuff. I hope it's not bothering you."

"Oh, no! Absolutely fine."

"David has addictions."

"He's fine. He's very polite and subtle about it."

"Good. Thank you for understanding."

Suffice it to say that we had a great discussion all around. The food was quite adequate, but this dinner wasn't about food.

David dropped me off at the hotel. Sitting in his car, we talked for 15 minutes after he turned off his engine. We spoke about grammar, usage, favorite authors, and our budding friendship. He recommended that I read Don DeLillo and William Gass.

I told him he should discover Richard Grand White, the 19th century's version of William Safire. "His books aren't easy to find," I said.

"That doesn't matter. Tell me books you think I should know, and I'll get them."

"How do you do that?"

"Well, let's just say I have my ways."

The next day, at State Farm, the seminar went well. I found myself wishing that my new friend were there.

Among the dozen or so letters he wrote to me is a funny one from August 1, 2002, just after he had arrived in Southern California. He had just been awarded the Roy E. Disney professorship at Pomona College. I had sent David an essay about quitting smoking—a splendid piece by my good friend John Trimble—and he responded that when he had once tried to quit, he "was a good deal more miserable than it sounds like Trimble is (was)," adding: "This might be his time to quit. I await my own." The postcript I thought was hilarious: "P.S. I got this stationery as a going-away present from friends. I think there are little bug carcasses ground into it . . . ."

Our correspondence after that was sporadic. He'd write postcards, mostly, and I'd write letters. I fear he may have written more frequently than I did.

We spoke briefly on the phone a few times. We both had busy lives. I invited him to my

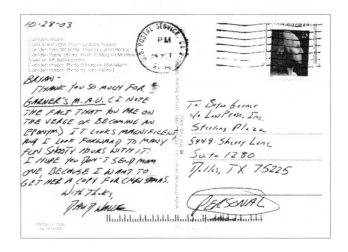

L.A. seminars from time to time, but scheduling always proved to be a problem.

In December 2004 I started videotaping interviews with state and federal judges, as well as a few writers such as James J. Kilpatrick, Nicholas Lemann, John Simon, and Brian Freeman. By January 2006, I'd conducted more than 100 of these interviews. That month, I called David to suggest that we do an interview in L.A. after one of my seminars if he had the evening available. He said it might be a two-hour drive each way, but he agreed. Very generous of him. When he arrived, it was only our second meeting—but it was as if we were old friends.

He said his agent had urged him not to do the interview. "Why?" I asked.

"Because you'll have complete control of it."

"Well, I will. But I hope you'll trust me."

We were at the Hilton Checkers Hotel in downtown L.A. We went to the second floor, where I had my impromptu studio set up. I turned on the camera, and we spoke for 67 minutes on tape.

It was a great interview, I thought then—and still do think. See for yourself in the pages that follow.

Then I suggested dinner. "Sure," he said, and we trudged up the hill to McCormick & Schmick's, just near 400 South Hope Street. He told me how happily married he was, and

I confessed how unhappily married I was. We were candid with each other, and I told him I was contemplating divorce—how for many years I had felt trapped in an intolerable situation.

After hearing my plight, he encouraged me to file for divorce, and by August I would do just that. It was a time of great upheaval in my otherwise fairly steady life. David was a great listener, and he gave good counsel.

To my lasting regret, my own problems overswayed the conversation that evening. His problems, to which he repeatedly referred in the past tense, seemed to be very distantly behind him. He loved teaching at Pomona, he was in a wonderful relationship with a wonderful wife that I'd soon meet (though I never did), and he wanted to know how he could help me.

Upon parting that evening, David said: "Okay, so you've enveloped me in this much of your narrative. You must tell me how the narrative plays out. You'll keep me informed. Agreed?"

"Agreed."

And so I did, a little. Not a blow-by-blow, but the highlights. But David grew less and less communicative. I didn't know whether it was something I might have said. Of course, I now know it wasn't.

B y the end of 2006, Justice Antonin Scalia and I had agreed to coauthor a book on advocacy. David had played a role even in that development.

Shortly after David's interview, I had decided to try interviewing Supreme Court justices—a venture that proved most challenging. In April, I wrote to Justice Scalia, who promptly declined an interview but invited me to have breakfast next time I was to be in Washington. That ended up being late June, right before the end of the Supreme Court term. Our breakfast took place at the Four Seasons in Georgetown, and we were joined by my daughter Caroline, then an undergraduate at Yale.

"There's a word for people like you and me," Justice Scalia said—"people who care a lot about good usage. What's the word? Oh, gosh!"

"Snoots?"

"Yes! That's it. There's a great essay in *Harper's* where this guy wrote a tremendous essay about it. My son, who's getting a Ph.D. in English, put me onto it."

"David Foster Wallace?"

"Yes! That's the guy. What a great essay."

"That essay is about my book on American usage."

"Really? Well, your stock's just gone way up in my mind."

No kidding. Within minutes, Justice Scalia had agreed to an interview. Soon seven other

Supreme Court justices would also agree. The Scalia interview took place on October 2, 2006. On the way back to Dallas afterward, I wrote him a letter proposing that we coauthor a book. Little did I know that Scalia's son Christopher, the English Ph.D., would be at home when my letter arrived.

"Dad! You get to write a book with Bryan Garner? Unbelievable."

Justice Scalia said yes.

That was a very direct result of "Tense Present." No doubt about it.

Two months later I learned that Justice Scalia would be visiting the Claremont Colleges. "You must meet David Foster Wallace," I said. At my urging, he asked his secretary to request from the college administration a meeting with David. I called David and left a message that he could expect an invitation to a Scalia event, and I suggested that he attend.

The Scalias and Wallaces ended up sitting together at a luncheon in February 2007. Both sides told me how thoroughly enjoyable the experience was. I was happy to have introduced them.

Shortly after, David left a voicemail message at my office. A secretary recorded it for me, and it remained for a long time on my iPod (until I lost it). It went something like this: "This is David

Wallace. I'm a friend of Mr. Garner's—I really am. You can ask him. Anyway, I just wanted to thank him for arranging the introduction with Justice Scalia and to say hello. I don't know who's going to get this message, but it's for real. I really am a friend of Bryan Garner. Again, it's David Wallace. Thanks."

We soon spoke with each other. He said that he was astonished at and slightly confused by how much he liked Justice Scalia—despite their political differences. He asked about the progress of my divorce, which entailed a new kind of high drama each week. I gave just a brief rundown, and he thanked me for the update. I thanked him for his friendship.

A couple of months later, I wrote to congratulate him on the cameo appearance of *Consider the Lobster* on the television show *Entourage*. He didn't reply.

At both of our dinners—in Bloomington and then in L.A.—I took a few books for David to sign. On all six of them, he did something that made me uncomfortable: he crossed out his name on the title page and wrote it in himself. I almost said something to him about it, to remark on what the crossing-out meant to me, but I refrained. It seemed inappropriately lugubrious, and it was surely a false notion I'd harbored since adolescence.

You see, at the age of 14 or 15, in Amarillo, I discovered a book on handwriting analysis. Within a few months I had pretty well memorized the book along with my childhood friend J.P. Allen, and the two of us were constantly asked to analyze our classmates' and others' handwriting. Occasionally we'd even be paid for it. Although I've never put much stock in its particular conclusions, I've always believed that some of the broader generalizations might hold true.

In any event, the crossing-out made me uncomfortable because of what that's supposed to suggest. Many people sign their names and then loop back through them, as if to underline or to cross a *t* or two, but instead mark directly through their names. This unpleasant habit is said to indicate self-destructiveness or suicidal tendencies.* So I've never liked seeing my own

---

*As a teenager, I learned this bit of graphological lore from M.N. Bunker, *Handwriting Analysis: The Art and Science of Reading Character by Graphoanalysis* (1959). Many others in this arguably pseudoscientific field have repeated the point. *See, e.g.,* Billie Pesin Rosen, *The Science of Handwriting Analysis* 188 (1965) ("Self-destructive tendencies are also indicated in signatures where the stroke, instead of turning towards the right, turns leftwards and slashes across the name itself."); Claude Santoy, *The ABCs of Handwriting Analysis* 143 (2005) ("crossed out signature (suicidal wishes)"); Treyce d'Gabriel, *The Only Handwriting Book You Will Ever Need* 283 (2008) (signature "crossed out by 'x' or angular paraph—he is vindictive and self-destructive to the point of fatality. He has suicidal tendencies . . . .").

Consider the Lobster and Other Essays

For Bryan A. Garner in friendship

~~David Foster Wallace~~

LITTLE, BROWN AND COMPANY
NEW YORK   BOSTON

name crossed out, by me or anyone else. In David's case, I particularly disliked the looped "delete" mark that proofreaders use. I chalked up my discomfort to superstition and decided to say nothing. David was a famous writer, and doubtless this was his habitual way of inscribing books. Indeed it was: a quick look at Google Images confirms that he always signed books this way.

In London, I recently discovered an inscribed E.M. Forster book in which Forster did the same thing—crossing out the printed name and autographing the title page. So maybe there's nothing to the thoughts I've just expressed; it may just be a literary convention among some authors. Yet in the collection of 200-plus inscribed books I was examining in London, Forster was alone in using this convention.

I learned of the sad news of David's suicide from the television—again and again. It still makes me morose to think about it, with the lingering fear that I should have, might have, been a better friend to David. I might have insisted that he keep me apprised of *his* narrative. If only I had.

But I know these are idle, worthless thoughts at this point.

Sometimes, when I'm unhappy, I'll read David's commencement speech immortalized in the booklet *This Is Water*. Or I'll read the interview you're now holding. And it makes me happier—happier to know that there was such a man, such a mind, such a friend. His words uplift me. They give me hope. I'm not alone. Strange, isn't it, that he didn't find the hope within himself—the hope he gave to so many others.

But he will continue to give us the hope of deep humanity, profound caring, and true understanding. That's the essence of David's enduring legacy.

و   و   و

People have asked me why I've waited so long to do anything with this interview—or to write a tribute to David. I've suffered from a kind of mental block. I haven't wanted to face it.

And I've wanted to be sure I was doing right by David's memory. In the end, I settled on having the royalties from this book dedicated to the Harry Ransom Center in Austin, which holds David's literary archives. I'm establishing a fund to support the care of his papers and the acquisition of still more of David's original work, if it can be found.

In the end, that's my best judgment in the matter.

ﻭ   *ﻭ*   *ﻭ*

I never spoke to David about his e-mail address: ocapmycap@[etc.—the providers varied]. The 1865 Walt Whitman poem, written to honor Lincoln, must have had special meaning to David—as it did (and does) to me. The elegy takes on even more meaning knowing that David adopted it as his online moniker:

> O Captain! My Captain! our fearful trip is done;
> The ship has weather'd every rack, the prize we sought
>   is won;
> The port is near, the bells I hear, the people all exulting,
> While follow eyes the steady keep, the vessel grim and
>   daring:
>
> > But O heart! heart! heart!
> > O the bleeding drops of red,
> > Where on the deck my Captain lies,
> > Fallen cold and dead.
>
> O Captain! my Captain! rise up and hear your bells;
> Rise up—for you the flag is flung—for you the bugle trills;
> For you the bouquets and ribbon'd wreaths—for you the
>   shores a-crowding;
> For you they call, the swaying mass, the eager faces
>   turning;
>
> > O Captain! dear father!
> > This arm beneath your head;

It is some dream that on the deck,
You've fallen cold and dead.

My Captain still does not answer, his lips are pale and still;
My father does not feel my arm, he has no pulse nor will;
The ship is anchor'd safe and sound, its voyage closed and
    done;
From fearful trip, the victor ship, comes in with object
    won.

Exult, O shores, and ring, O bells!
But I, with mournful tread,
Walk the deck my captain lies,
Fallen cold and dead.

B.A.G.
September 2013

Quack
This
Way

David Foster Wallace &
Bryan A. Garner Talk
Language and Writing

An interview conducted
on February 3, 2006
in the Hilton Checkers Hotel,
Los Angeles, California

The reader cannot read your mind.

BAG: David, what's the best way to learn to write well, in your view?

DFW: And I ask you to define "write well." I noodled over it before.

BAG: You talk about writing well in your essay "Authority and American Usage," in *Consider the Lobster*. What does it mean to write well?

DFW: In the broadest possible sense, writing well means to communicate clearly and interestingly and in a way that feels alive to the reader. Where there's some kind of relationship between the writer and the reader—even though it's mediated by a kind of text—there's an electricity about it.

That's very general, but . . .

BAG: How does somebody learn to do that?

DFW: [*pause*] Well, there are standard things you say, like, "You read a lot" and "You practice a lot." Questions like this I field more as a schoolteacher than as a writer. In my experience with students— talented students of writing—the most important thing for them to remember is that someone who is not them and cannot read their mind is going to have to read this. In order to write effectively, you don't pretend it's a letter to some individual you know, but you never forget that what you're engaged in is a communication to another human being. The bromide associated with this is that the reader cannot read your mind. *The reader cannot read your mind.* That would be the biggest one.

Probably the second biggest one is learning to pay attention in different ways. Not just reading a lot, but paying attention to the way the sentences are put together, the clauses are joined, the way the sentences go to make up a paragraph. Exercises as boneheaded as you take a book you really like, you read a page of it three, four times, put it down, and then try to imitate it word for word so that you can feel your own muscles trying to achieve some of the effects that the page of text you like did. If you're like me, it will be in your failure to be able to duplicate it that you'll actually learn what's going on.

Now I'm going to stop for a second. Is that an example of what you want?

BAG: That's fantastic.

DFW: Where does one look in the camera? It feels as if I'm catatonic and I'm staring at a point in space.

BAG: You can just look at me.

DFW: Okay.

BAG: Robert Louis Stevenson wrote in his little collection of essays—I think it came out posthumously—*Learning to Write*, about how he would do just what you said: take a passage from a book, read it, reread it, reread it, put it down, and try to replicate it.

DFW: Oh, really?

BAG: Yeah!

DFW: I thought I made that up.

BAG: Did you really?

DFW: Well, the students just roll their eyes when you say it to them. It sounds really, really stupid, but in fact, you can read a page of text, right? And "Oh, that was pretty good . . . ," but you don't get any sense of the infinity of choices that were made in that text until you start trying to reproduce them. And so that was just a random exercise that I could think of. I didn't know other people . . . I know James Jones had a writing teacher who made them retype great books, but I think the book was right there and they were just retyping. They were supposed to learn through their hands, or something kind of flaky.

BAG: So you don't put much stock in that, the mechanical typing of it, as opposed to really mentally trying to recreate something?

DFW: Here though, I mean I'm 43, and we get into the weird age thing because for my students, many of whom compose on a typewriter, that might actually be a useful exercise. The *writing* writing that I do is longhand.

BAG: You write everything in longhand?

DFW: Well, the first two or three drafts are always longhand, yeah. Only because

I went through this school where they made me write a lot and it was right before computers became ubiquitous. And I just find that it makes me . . . I can type very much faster than I can write. And writing makes me slow down in a way that helps me pay attention. Like, is the clause that I just . . . does this make sense, what I just said? Which is very difficult, at least for me, to keep in mind when I'm actually writing the thing, unless something slows me down.

BAG: So when you do a draft, will you actually do a second draft, recopying and supplementing, adding, embellishing?

DFW: For what I would consider caviar work, like my own work that's really important to me, yeah. But that's a device that I picked up as a sophomore in college, where I had these philosophy classes where you had to turn in five-page papers once a week, and I just found that I couldn't do it unless I recopied it several times because there was just too much different stuff to think about.

I don't know whether that would be helpful to anyone else, particularly computer jockeys. I don't know how they would really do it. My students have never successfully explained it to me. I don't think they do drafts, actually. Which doesn't mean that the better of them don't go back, look, tweak, move stuff around, add stuff, and take stuff out. What is a draft to them isn't necessarily a draft to me.

BAG: To what extent do you think you had an advantage as a writer because your mother teaches writing and grammar?

DFW: I think people have an edge whose parents read a lot and grow up in a kind of culture of reading. Mom's brainwashing of us tended to concern spoken English a lot more, right? You know, "Can Johnny and me go to the park?" "No." You know, the whole drill.

Writing-wise, I know I've heard you talk about some of the stuff you do with your kids. Your kids are much better sports than I. When my mom would start to tear apart . . . See, even the way I say it . . . something . . . I would get so angry that early on—13, 14—she quit doing it. I was a good student in high school, but it was a big public high school. I was kind of a jock. I had various illicit activities.

BAG: Tennis player.

DFW: Yeah. But I hung with jocks and I hung with people whose interests were extra-curricular and chemical, if you know what I mean. I went from there to Amherst College, this little, elite . . . It's a very good school, but one reason it's good is they work your hiney off, and so it was there that I learned that . . . .

All right, I now teach at a school somewhat like Amherst, but I came there from a kind of reasonable, midlevel public school. And the big challenge that I found teaching writing to students there, even the bright ones, was the difference between expressive writing and communicative writing.

It was in college—particularly when I had professors who didn't just put letters on the paper, but would, in fact, write mini-letters of response—that I realized that my papers were intended to be communications. Whereas in high school—and I don't know whether this is still the case—it seems to me that the paradigm is more expressive. "We want the kids to write. Writing is good. It's good because you wrote it. Share yourself with me." And to the extent that I understand it . . . in the real writing world, one of the axioms is that the reader doesn't care about you. You know, the fact that this is you means absolutely nothing to them. The fact is, what can they get from this document that is going to require time, and perhaps money, for them to read? It's a very different paradigm to come at writing from. And I snapped to it perhaps late—it wasn't until college. Probably bright, well-educated high-school students are starting to catch onto that.

But the difference between expressive writing and communicative writing is . . . I don't usually say it that way in class because that's kind of jargon a little bit. But there's a real difference between writing where you're communicating to somebody, the same way I'm trying to communicate with you, versus writing that's almost a well-structured diary entry where the point is [*singing*] "This is me, this is me!" and it's going out into the world.

One of the things that the college drummed into me is, "Welcome to the adult world. It doesn't care about you. You want it to? Make it. Make it care."

BAG: So readers are essentially selfish, or at least self-interested, and they need to get something out of the writing. Is that part of it?

DFW: I certainly don't talk to students that way. What I talk about is that one of the things that's good about writing and practicing writing is it's a great remedy for my natural self-involvement and self-centeredness. Right? "I am the center of my own world, my thoughts and feelings are more immediate, therefore . . . ." I mean we all know the drill, right? When students snap to the fact that there's such a thing as a really bad writer, a pretty good writer, a great writer—when they start wanting to get better—they start realizing that really learning how to write effectively is, in fact, probably more of a matter of spirit than it is of intellect. I think probably even of verbal facility. And the spirit means I never forget there's someone on the end of the line, that I owe that person certain allegiances, that I'm sending that person all kinds of messages, only some of which have to do with the actual content of what it is I'm trying to say.

BAG: How much can you tell me . . .

DFW: You know that I'm now reprising certain stuff that's in the article?

BAG: That's great, though.

DFW: Okay, but you don't mind that?

BAG: No, no, no.

DFW: Okay.

BAG: So how much can you tell about a person from his or her writing?

DFW: You mean a student?

BAG: A student . . . anybody.

DFW: Well, if you're talking about reading a book . . . I mean, most people that are publishing books are pros, P-R-O-S, and they've got editors.

Let me give you an example. A lot of the classes I teach now, they're these fiction workshops, you know, touchy-feely, yadda yadda yadda. Well, what we in my class end up spending a lot of time on is writing the letters of response to the person who's written the story. And the key term is supposed to be *helpfulness*, which is neither mean nor nice. But as a rhetorical template, the idea is, "How am I helpful to the author? How can I give the author a sense of what this was like for me to read it and how it might be made better?"

I'll find very often the students have no problem with the niceness. They're very good with compliments; they're very good at stroking the author. But they tend to lapse into various things, and the younger they are, the more inclined they are to do this. They talk about what the experience for them was like reading it—"Well, it reminded me of the time my Aunt Rose cooked a meal like that"—and will almost lapse into its own narrative. I'm giving you a very stark example, but the examples . . . You say to them, "No, no. This is not the job. This may be an interesting factoid, but your job here is to communicate stuff to the author about the author's text. Forget about you. Right? Talk about what in the text reminded you of that story. Don't tell the author that story. It's not appropriate."

And even for very bright freshmen and sophomores, what I've noticed is that this is an enormous shock to them. This is, "I am not, in and of myself, interesting to a reader. If I want to seem interesting, work has to be done in order to make myself interesting." It's stuff that these kids understand socially very easily. Right? They know you don't pick somebody up for a date without showering or brushing your teeth . . . are monosyllabic the whole night . . . stare straight ahead. Why don't you do that? Because you look like a schmo, right? But you're you. You're sharing your presence, right? So I'm telling you that because that's usually the analogy that I give them for this stuff.

I don't know why I'm making broad gestures.

BAG: It's great though. This is fantastic.

DFW: This is okay?

BAG: Yeah. I love this.

DFW: You're very polite; I have no idea whether to believe you. We'll soldier on.

BAG: Well, how good as writers are bright college students? Can you generalize? How far do they have to go?

DFW: Well, I would need to know according to what sort of measuring stick. How close would they be to being able to do it professionally?

BAG: Yeah.

DFW: I don't think any of them could do it professionally. But there are 70 million different kinds of professional writing. I'm sorry. The question just makes my brain shut down, I don't know what you mean.

BAG: Well, I mean it as kind of an open-ended thing. You're right, there are all these different paths . . . .

DFW: Oh, this is part of an exhortation to work hard, then.

BAG: A little bit.

DFW: Okay.

BAG: How far do they have to go? I mean, don't you think a lot of your students at Pomona probably come in thinking they're really quite good writers, and they have to be disabused of that notion?

DFW: Well, but it gets tricky. Many of them are quite good high-school writers, or college-freshmen writers. Right? Probably the smart thing to say is this: there's a certain amount of stuff about writing that's like music or math or certain kinds of sports. Some people really have a knack for this, we've all seen this. As Will Hunting says in *Good Will Hunting*, "They sit down at the piano and it just makes sense to them." Right?

One of the exciting things about teaching college is you see a couple of them every semester. They're not always the best writers in the room because the other part of it is it takes a heck of a lot of practice. Gifted, really really gifted writers pick stuff up quicker, but they also usually have a great deal more ego invested in what they write and tend to be more difficult to teach.

One runs across this more with graduate students than with undergrads, but the fact of the matter is that good writing isn't a science. It's an art, and the horizon is infinite. You can always get better. If what you mean is "able to be a graceful benefit to a profession in which writing is crucial"—academia, the law, medicine, journalism—many of them are right on track.

But it's also the case with the kind of classes I teach that a great many of them won't be doing writing as you or I understand writing. However, they will be reading. They will be thinking about professional and political issues. They will be communicating to other people.

It's true, I think, that a lot of the muscles you use, skills you use, in trying to get better as a writer, are skills and muscles that pay off in ways that don't immediately seem to have to do with writing simply because language and interpersonal communication is to a large extent . . . it's our world, right?

Yeah. That wandered afield, but that's probably . . .

Crummy, turgid, verbose, abstruse, abstract, solecism-ridden prose.

BAG: Let's talk about writers and readers for a second. What if I were to tell you that a lot of lawyers say to me they're writing for judges who themselves don't write very well, who write a lot of jargon-laden stuff, so they think the best expressive tactic then is to mimic the style of the judges for whom they are writing? Does that make sense to you?

DFW: This gets very tricky. The same thing happens in academia. When students enter my classes, very often what I end up doing is beating out of them habits they were rewarded for in high school—many of them having to do with excessive abstraction, wordiness, overcomplication, excessive reliance on jargon, especially in literary criticism.

But it gets tricky because they will point out that some of the other professors in the department appear to expect this kind of writing. It's the sort of prose in which their syllabus and handouts are written. So to a certain extent, it's tricky. What I say to these students is, "Between you and me, different people have different levels of skill at writing." Somebody like a judge or a professor who is himself [*whispering*] kind of a shitty writer is nevertheless usually a really good reader. And he or she will not necessarily make the number of connections you're worried about when you worry that "If I turn in this pellucid, lapidary marvel, somehow the judge won't like it because it's not like the judge's own style." I would say if judges are like profs, 99% of them will reward you for clarity, for precision, for minimizing the unnecessary effort they have to make. And it probably won't occur to them that it would be a *darned* good idea to incorporate some of these principles into their own writing because some people are just dumb as writers. So that is an argument, I think, for: Regardless of whom you're writing for or what you think about the current debased state of the English language, right?—in which the President says things that would embarrass a junior-high-school student—the fact remains that, particularly in the professions, that the average person you're writing for is an acute, sensitive, attentive, sophisti-cated reader who will appreciate adroit-ness, precision, economy, and clarity. Not always, but I think the vast majority of the time.

BAG: I often answer that question in terms of fiction and say, "Even though almost nobody in this room could create a first-rate novel, that doesn't mean that we, as consumers of novels, would want to go out and buy mediocre novels with a muddled story line. We still can appreciate a good novel." Does that analogy make sense?

DFW: Yeah. Well, there are all kinds of goodness in terms of novels, if you're talking about commercial versus literary, but I understand the point. I see the point that you're making. And it is true. The side issue is the fact that a lot of professors and college writing teachers are themselves, in English and in the other departments, atrociously bad writers. In my experience, the only downside of that is that they're not very skillful editors of student papers and are not apt to be able to give them helpful suggestions for making their writing better. It does not mean that students will be punished for writing good, clear, well-organized papers.

BAG: Why do so many English professors write so poorly?

DFW: [*long pause*] A lot of academic writing—and my guess is a lot of legal, medical, scientific writing—is done by . . . [*pause*] All right. How to do this . . . [*long pause, clicking tongue*]

The simple way to put it, I think, is: Writing, like any kind of communicating, is complicated. When you're writing a document for your professional peers, you're sending out a whole lot of different messages. Some of them are the stuff you're arguing; some of them are stuff about you.

My guess is that disciplines that are populated by smart, well-educated people who are good readers but are nevertheless characterized by crummy, turgid, verbose, abstruse, abstract, solecism-ridden prose, are usually part of a discipline where the dynamic between writing as a vector of meaning—as a way to get information or opinion from me to you—versus writing as maybe a form of dress or speech or style or etiquette that signals that "I am a member of this group" gets thrown off.

There's the kind of boneheaded explanation, which is that a lot of people with PhDs are stupid, and like many stupid people, they associate complexity with intelligence. And therefore they get brainwashed into making their stuff more complicated than it needs to be. I think the smarter thing to say is that in many tight, insular communities— where membership is partly based on intelligence, proficiency, and being able to speak the language of the discipline— pieces of writing become as much or more about presenting one's own qualifications for inclusion in the group than transmission of meaning. And that's how in disciplines like academia—or, I've read some really good legal prose, but when it's really, really horrible (IRS Code stuff)—I think that very often it stems from insecurity and that people feel that unless they can mimic the particular jargon and style of their peers, they won't be taken seriously, and their ideas won't be taken seriously. It's a guess. It's somewhat parroting you too, I believe, so you'll like it.

BAG: I've got to ask you this question: Why do people . . . We haven't even gotten to the second question on my list yet, but . . .

DFW: Well, you've jumped around a bit.

BAG: Why, in your view, do people use vogue words?

DFW: Well, we should first concede that a good 60% of the current English vocabulary started as vogue words. So your term *vogue words* is slightly pejorative in a way I sympathize with, but it's a bit of a loaded question. Probably it has to do with the fact that in speaking and writing, again, an enormous number of different kinds of communication are spraying out all over the place.

Vogue words, with the classic example being various code, slang words you and your teenage set used, inexplicable to the adults around you, are a quick and easy way to signify membership in a particular kind of group—what scholars would call a discourse community. On another level, when a vogue word—*to dialogue, to proactively dialogue*, or something—when it enters the mainstream, I think it becomes trendy because a great deal of listening, talking, and writing for many people takes place below the level of consciousness. It happens very fast. They don't pay it very much attention, and they've heard it a lot. It kind of enters into the nervous system. They get the idea, without it ever being conscious, that this is the good, current, credible way to say this, and they spout it back. And for people outside, say, the corporate business world or the advertising world, it becomes very easy to make fun of this kind of stuff. But in fact, probably if we look carefully at ourselves and the way we're constantly learning language . . .

I've been married a year, and I see it just with my wife. She'll use a word in a joking way that I appreciate, and three days later I'll repeat it back to her so we get a little giggle that the two of us can share. And then after a while, we've built this strange vocabulary of English words, but that have connotations private to us. It's a way to cohere, right? What's interesting . . . Well, in a marriage you don't share your little language, so there's no one to irritate. Vogue words tend to irritate people who aren't in the group that the vogue words are meant to signal inclusion with, possibly because part of their whole point is to exclude people who aren't in that group.

BAG: So if you and your wife were doing this with a dinner for six with each other, it *would* irritate others who felt excluded?

DFW: Yeah. The puzzle is why, in a kind of mass national sense, we don't have that sense of self-consciousness about it—that more people don't think that when I say *to proactively dialogue,* and I could really probably say *to speak* or *converse,* it's really somewhat silly. It takes time and attention for that to occur to you. And a lot of us . . . I mean this is not a . . . I'm a snooty guy, so I'm judging a little bit—it's sort of inevitable. A lot of us are very sloppy in the way that we use language. And another advantage of learning to write better, whether or not you want to do it for a living, is that it makes you pay more attention to this stuff. The downside is stuff begins bugging you that didn't bug you before. If you're in the express lane and it says, "10 Items or Less," you will be bugged because *less* is actually inferior to *fewer* for items that are countable. So you can end up being bugged a lot of the time.

But it is still, I think, well worth paying attention. And it does help, I think . . . the more attention one pays, the more one is immune to the worst excesses of vogue words, slang, you know. Which really I think on some level for a lot of listeners or readers, if you use a whole lot of it, you just kind of look like a sheep—somebody who isn't thinking, but is parroting . . . I know all that is going to get trimmed out. I couldn't figure out how to make the last bit fit with the rest.

BAG: What do you think about middle-aged people who adopt the current teenage slang? You've seen it. I've seen it.

DFW: Sure.

BAG: You must analyze this.

DFW: I don't analyze it, but I think we've all noticed it and we've all noticed the kind of sneering amusement that it occasions. There's something pathetic about it. What's interesting is why it's pathetic. It's pathetic because somebody who's older is, by definition, not a member of the set of a bunch of teenagers who are sitting around doing MTV-speak. Right? It's pathetic because it's knocking on a door that nobody's going to open. Right? It's pathetic the same way that Rudolph's saying, "Can I play the reindeer games?"

and they're going, "No, no, no, go away"
is. It's pathetic in that the person that's
trying it is kind of a schlemiel. And
we love to laugh at pathetic schlemiels,
particularly who are trying to look the
opposite of that. Right? People who are
attempting to signal . . . well, *social climber*
would be the old-fashioned term. Right?
We reserve a special kind of amused
scorn for people who are trying to signal
inclusion in a group to which they do not
rightfully belong.

This is why people who speak or
write poorly in the form of hypercorrection, and in that case make errors—
"Throw the ball to Bryan and I," or
something—on the level of my nervous
system, bug me a whole lot more than
if somebody from my hometown says,
"Hey, can Bryan and me come over and
watch TV?" Right? Because the person
who misuses what they think is the
correct *I* is trying to signal a level of
sophistication through which signal
they are . . . Ah, see, I'm putting it too
abstrusely. They're trying to signal a level

of linguistic sophistication to which they have just shown they are not entitled. Right?

BAG: Right.

DFW: So yeah . . . which you would be able to put much more succinctly.

BAG: I doubt it. Is it true easy writing is cursed hard reading? Does writing well always involve hard work?

DFW: I don't mean to be slippery, Does writing good e-mails take a lot of work? I mean, certain kinds of writing well—writing letters, writing e-mails, maybe writing corporate memos that just involve either a high degree of informality or a certain three or four skills—no, aren't very hard to do. Writing well in the sense of writing something interesting and urgent and alive, that actually has calories in it for the reader—the reader walks away having benefited from the 45 minutes she put into reading the thing—maybe isn't hard for a certain few. I mean, maybe John Updike's first drafts are these incredible . . . Apparently Bertrand Russell could just simply sit down and do this. I don't know anyone who can do that. For me, the cliché that "Writing that appears effortless takes the most work" has been borne out through very unpleasant experience.

BAG: How hard have you had to work to get where you are as a writer?

DFW: [*long pause*] On the level about which you and I are talking, this kind of thing, I consider myself about a journeyman. Right? So the larger lesson would be, okay, somebody else looking at me, "He gets to write books for a living. He must be very, very good."

[*aside*] Okay, I'm not doing a good job. See, because it's going to look like I'm just modestly kicking at the ground, and that's not what it means . . . It means . . .

Like any art, probably, the more experience you have with it, the more the horizon of what being really good is . . . the more it recedes. So a great deal of now being in my 40s and having done this pretty seriously for 20 years is I now have a much better idea of the ways in which I'm not really very good. Which you could say is an important part of my education as a writer. If I'm not aware of some deficits, I'm not going to be working hard to try to overcome them.

My main deficit, at least in terms of nonfiction prose, is I have difficulty of being as clear as I want to be. I have various tricks for working around that and making it kind of charming to watch somebody trying to be clear, but the fact of the matter is, I can't be clear and compressed in the way that, say, parts of the preface of your dictionary that I liked very much are clear and compressed.

And I have a strange phobia that there's a crucial point and I haven't transmitted it satisfactorily, so I have to say it again a different way and then later on again a different way. And I think I lean . . . There's a Poe thing, right? "One out of one hundred things is discussed at great length because it really is obscure. Ninety-nine out of one hundred things are obscure because they're discussed at more length than they need to be." And so, for me right now, because I just got done editing a nonfiction book, I'm very well in touch with the ways in which I'm not as good as I would like to be.

On the other hand, I'm way, way better than I was 20 years ago. But I don't know that I'm a very good example because I'm somebody who got to do this for a living, meaning I spent massive amounts of time and drafts and noodling over this stuff in a way that the ordinary writing American wouldn't get to, or even really want to. Right? Any more than, you know, somebody who wants to be a basketball player is going to shoot free-throws over and over and over again in a way that would bore you and me out of our minds.

So I guess the larger message is that it becomes very tempting to go, "Oh, what's good? Okay, look at that guy over there: that's good." Just be aware that that guy is looking at other people and going, "No, no, *that's* good." And like any kind of infinitely rich art, or any infinitely rich medium, like language, the possibilities for improvement are infinite and so are the possibilities for screwing up and ceasing to be good in the ways you want to be good.

Is that better?

BAG: Who are the writers that have come closest to reaching a kind of nirvana, in your view? Are there any? I mean, maybe there are just too many different realms to talk about.

DFW: Well, and there are too many different languages. I mean, I'm talking just about in English. We're talking about fiction writers?

BAG: Fiction, nonfiction. What writers do you most admire?

DFW: You mean writers I think are models of incredibly clear, beautiful, alive, urgent, crackling-with-voltage prose?

BAG: Sure.

DFW: William Gass, Don DeLillo, Cynthia Ozick, Louise Erdrich when she's firing on all cylinders. Do you want me to name more if it means I have to sit and think a bit?

BAG: Sure.

DFW: Here's a weird one, though: one of my very favorites is Cormac McCarthy. Cormac McCarthy, particularly in a book like *Blood Meridian,* is writing an English very remote from our own. It's more like the King James Bible on acid, right? It's not any sort of way you or I would write. And yet what he is able to do with it and the effects he's able to create with it simply blow your hair back.

So probably the smart thing to say is, if you spend enough time reading or writing, you find a voice, but you also find certain tastes. You find certain writers who when they write, it makes your own brain voice like a tuning fork, and you just resonate with them. And when that happens, reading those writers—not all of whom are modern . . . I mean, if you are willing to make allowances for the way English has changed, you can go way, way back with this—becomes a source of unbelievable joy. It's like eating candy for the soul.

And I sometimes have a hard time understanding how people who don't have that in their lives make it through the day. But it's also true that my father can listen to classical music and be nourished in ways that I'll never understand. Or my wife can go to some local gallery and look at art and come home looking . . . she's a different person. It's not just that she looks different. She's been changed somehow.

So probably the smart thing to say is that lucky people develop a relationship with a certain kind of art that becomes spiritual, almost religious, and doesn't mean, you know, church stuff, but it means you're just never the same. You're smiling. That's your experience too, right?

BAG: Yeah, it is, it is very much.

DFW: Do you have a hard time understanding how people who don't have that live?

BAG: Yes.

DFW: But lots of people don't.

BAG: I think most people don't. And I think most people don't have a kind of zealous passion for anything in particular. But I think it probably demands a kind of sensitivity to art.

DFW: [*grimacing*] Do you think that's true? I don't think there's a person alive who doesn't have certain passions. I think if you're lucky, either by genetics or you just get a really good education, you find things that become passions that are just really rich and really good and really joyful, as opposed to the passion being, you know, getting drunk and watching football. Which has its appeals, right? But it is not the sort of calories that get you through your 20s, and then your 30s, and then your 40s, and, "Ooh, here comes death," you know, the big stuff.

BAG: But some people that I know . . . I know lawyers in their 40s who are trying to figure out what they like and what they want to do with their lives.

DFW: There are probably people like that.

It's also true that we go through cycles. Right? At least in terms of my own work, I've gone through three or four of these, and I'm in one now, where it feels as if I've forgotten everything I've ever known. I have no idea what to do.

Most of what I want to do seems to me like I've done it before. It seems stupid.

And except on the days I'm really depressed, I realize that I've been through these before. These are actually good—one's being larval. I'm being larval, right? Or else, I just can't do this anymore, in which case I'll find something else to do. And I brood about that a fair amount.

But I think the hard thing to distinguish among my friends is who . . . who's the 45-year-old who doesn't know what she likes or what she wants to do? Is she immature? Or is she somebody who's getting reborn over and over and over again? In a way, that's rather cool.

BAG: Could be that. Could be.

DFW: But yeah, we both know immature schmucks. It's also a really great way to create drama in your life, right? "I don't know what I like."

BAG: I suppose so.

DFW: "I have to find myself," etc., etc.

BAG: When you're writing nonfiction, how do you go about research and then organizing your thoughts when you're writing a long essay?

DFW: I find it very difficult. The truth is that most of the nonfiction pieces I do are at least partly experiential. They involve going to a place, talking to people, taking notes. My fondest wish is that no one would have the kind of process I have with it. I end up taking a hundred times more notes than I need.

My first draft usually approximates somebody in the midst of an epileptic seizure. It's usually about the second or the third draft where I begin having any idea of actually what this thing is about. So my own way of doing it, it's not very economical in terms of time. It is just doing it over and over and over again and throwing stuff away and, you know, whining and crying to friends and stuff and then going back and trying it over again. I think there are very few professional writers—and certainly very few people who are doing things like having to supply good briefs or opinions in the law—who would want to or could afford to go through a process like that.

My process appears to be getting precipitate out of an enormous amount of solution. I wish it weren't. I heartily advise people not to develop a process like that. I can get away with it because I don't do many nonfiction pieces. I couldn't make a living doing them because just one takes me six months.

The trunk cable into the linguistic heart.

BAG: I remember your first letter to me about the usage piece you wrote. You said, I think, you'd spent three months straight on that essay.

DFW: Well, it was supposed to be a book review, but it turned out there was no way to review your dictionary without talking about what the stakes were. Right? At the start, it was for the *New Republic* and the *New Republic* got tired of this very early on. And then I was just doing it for myself.

BAG: Speaking of usage books, what is the purpose of the usage dictionary? What is that kind of book for?

DFW: Give me some background. Give me some prep and then ask it again.

BAG: Most lawyers have never heard of the usage book—never heard of the usage dictionary. A lot of people who see *dictionary* assume, "Ah, this competes with *Webster's*, but I already have a *Webster's Dictionary*, so I don't need this." And they don't understand the concept of a usage book. So of what utility is a usage book to some writer—of fiction or nonfiction?

DFW: I urge my students to get a usage dictionary. I in fact plug yours, but I don't require them to get yours. If you don't have a prof who is urging you to do it, you're in a paradoxical situation. To recognize that you need a usage dictionary, you have to be paying a level of attention to your own writing that very few people are doing. If you are paying attention and you're like me, you will notice a phenomenon: there are certain words that we chronically misspell. There are certain words . . . *census*. I've looked the word up 10 times, but if I ever have *census* or *consensus* in something, damned if I don't have to go back to the dictionary and look it up again. Well, it's the same thing with *abstruse* versus *obtuse*, or what exactly are the four different ways that a comma can function in this sentence?

A usage dictionary is a little bit . . . I consider it kind of like a linguistic hard drive. To be honest, for me the big trio is a big dictionary, a usage dictionary, a thesaurus—only because I cannot retain and move nimbly around in enough of the language not to need these extra sources.

As a teacher, about 90% of my job is getting the students to understand why they might need one. And it involves teaching in a way that most college teachers don't teach when there is a usage error, or a two-way adverb, say, or *only* misplaced in a sentence, or a comma where there doesn't need to be one. Jesus! [*rolling eyes*] It means circling the error and explaining to the student why it's an error in the margins, which takes a lot of time. I teach only one class, so I do it.

I think people would be better off simply taking the advice of somebody like you. Everybody needs one of these things. Whether or not you use a usage dictionary, which gives general norms and guidelines for how different words work, how things that might appear to be synonyms in fact aren't—all kinds of stuff. The best dictionary going right now, as far as I can see, is yours— although if I were a Brit, maybe I'd like the new *Fowler's*, I don't know.

For me, very often it's used in, say, fifth or sixth drafts—not early on. I don't want to think about that stuff early on; I've got too many other things to think about. But as part of the revision, and particularly the editing and proofreading process, I just . . . since I was 23 years old . . . I don't see how anybody does

without an *OED* and a *Roget* and a good
usage dictionary.

BAG: But you must have internalized a lot
of the usage stuff, so that it comes out
pretty clean in the first draft.

DFW: Yeah, I mean, I'm not semiliterate, but
again, this is why I don't know if I'm a
good example. It would be easy for someone watching this to go, "Well, the guy's
obsessed, and this is his living. I don't
need . . ." The thing of it is, you bet—I've
internalized way more of the stuff than
the average person. But I'm also trying to
do things and mess around with syntax
and punctuation and create effects that
probably nobody even cares about.
Certainly most people aren't going to be
trying to do that in their writing.

But the fact of the matter is that
most people—literate, well-educated
people . . . There are a whole lot of
usage conventions and rules that unless
you're mnemonic, you're just not going
to have . . . I'd be willing to lay money

that in putting together your usage dictionary, you made use of an abundant number of other sources, and not just for examples of bad usage. There is no single human being who can do this.

Though one of the things I love about the usage dictionary—and it's not a lawbook. These aren't laws. But the *OED* and your book or the new *Fowler's* and *Roget*, a *recent Roget*—for me, it's like if all of English is a treasure and this is the chest that it's in. Right? I don't spend all my time reading these things, but it's there whenever I want it. And it can save me embarrassment, and I almost always learn something.

You'll cut this out, but a usage dictionary is one of the great bathroom books of *all* time. Because it has the appeal of trivia, the entries are for the most part brief, and you end up within 48 hours—due to that weird psychological effect—actually drawing on exactly what you learned in some weird, coincidental way. So the bathroom usage-dictionary plug is now on film.

BAG: Actually, my experience was the same; and I have frequently said that, but I always have to . . .

DFW: Bathroom? The bathroom?

BAG: Yeah!

DFW: Outstanding!

BAG: Yeah, to lawyers, and I always have to apologize a little bit about it. And some women come up and say, "We wish you'd stop talking about that; it's just too gross to contemplate." Maybe men can take that. I always get a couple.

DFW: For a fiction writer, there are other advantages. Like your book *Modern Legal Usage*. Right? Say you want to have a character who sounds reasonably like a lawyer. There are similar guides or resources available in most of the disciplines. It is the trunk cable into the linguistic heart of these disciplines.

BAG: Did you know *Modern Legal Usage* before you reviewed *Modern American Usage*?

DFW: No. I ended up ordering whatever edition was out at that time as part of my research on you. But no, uh-uh. I know Gaddis did, at least for *A Frolic of His Own*. He used it. Have you ever read, heard of it?

BAG: You recommended it to me once, along with DeLillo, and I went out and immediately bought all these books. And I have a little shelf of books that David Foster Wallace recommended.

DFW: Well, the fun thing is part of *A Frolic of His Own* involves a fake legal opinion about an abstract sculpture and whether it should be torn down because a child is trapped in it. It's not quite Learned Hand, but if you read some Learned Hand and then you read this, you can tell that the guy had access to some good legal usage—the guy's not a lawyer.

BAG: I've got to get further into the book.

DFW: Yeah, whatever. It's not even his best book, but it's a great example of, you know, if you're not Scott Turow or whatever and you don't have actual experience with the profession.

Never let the reader forget what the stakes are here.

BAG: When you're writing a long nonfiction piece, do you try to understand the structure of the whole before you begin writing sentences and paragraphs in earnest?

DFW: No.

BAG: Or do you write and then kind of fill it out as you go?

DFW: Everybody is different. I don't discover the structure except by writing sentences because I can't think structurally well enough. But I know plenty of good nonfiction writers. Some actually use Roman-numeral outlines, and they wouldn't even know how to begin without it.

If you really ask writers, at least most of the ones I know—and people are always interested and want to know what you do—most of them are habits or tics or superstitions we picked up between the ages of 15 and 25, often in school. I think at a certain point, part of one's linguistic nervous system gets hardened over that time or something, but it's all different.

I would think for argumentative writing it would be very difficult, at a certain point, not to put it into some kind of outline form.

Were it me, I see doing it in the third or fourth draft as part of the "Oh my God, is what I'm saying making any sense at all? Can somebody who's reading it, who can't read my mind, fit it into some sort of schematic structure of argument?"

I think a more sane person would probably do that at the beginning. But I don't know that anybody would be able to get away with . . . Put it this way: if you couldn't do it, if you can't put . . . If you're writing an argumentative thing, which I think people in your discipline are, if you couldn't, if forced, put it into an outline form, you're in trouble.

BAG: Whereas there probably are pieces of your nonfiction essays and reviews . . . Some of them are rather complex. If you tried to do an outline, would it work— after the fact?

DFW: Well, but I do very few straight-out argumentative things. The stuff that I do is part narrative, part argumentative, part meditative, part experiential. The closest I've come to actual argumentative pieces are book reviews, and I mean straight- out, you-got-300-words book reviews. And at a certain draft, at a certain point in those drafts, I always make an outline. But that's because I've got 300 words, which for me is very tight. How am I going to make it tight?

BAG: Do you teach argumentative writing at all?

DFW: I have. I mean, I have taught . . . . Do you mean in freshman comp, "Here are the rhetorical modes . . ."

BAG: In any form.

DFW: Mostly now, if I'm not teaching straight-out fiction writing or essay writing, I'm teaching lit. And most lit papers are argumentative, which is a shock to many students. But what you're really arguing for is something you must yourself create, which is an interesting reading of something.

But now my head's starting to race. Yes, that's my answer to your question. Yes, I have taught argumentative writing.

BAG: Let's take argumentative writing. Do you have a view of what a good opener should do, what you do in the middle, and what you do at the end?

DFW: [*pause*] For an argumentative piece . . . We're not talking, "Pretend I'm a legal writer," right?

BAG: No.

DFW: A good opener, first and foremost, fails to repel. Right? So it's interesting and engaging. It lays out the terms of the argument, and, in my opinion, should also in some way imply the stakes. Right? Not only am I right, but in any piece of writing there's a tertiary argument: why should you spend your time reading this? Right? "So here's why the following issue might be important, useful, practical." I would think that if one did it deftly, one could in a one-paragraph opening grab the reader, state the terms of the argument, and state the motivation for the argument. I imagine most good argumentative stuff that I've read, you could boil that down to the opener.

Is that . . . ? I'm looking at you now. We're a little out of my area here. I'm not a rhetorician. There's whole textbooks written about this stuff.

BAG: You're quite a rhetorician.

DFW: No, but I'm saying, like, how to teach it.

BAG: Yeah.

DFW: That would be my guess.

BAG: What do you do in the middle?

DFW: I'm sorry?

BAG: What do you do in the middle part of an argumentative piece?

DFW: You're talking about the body of the piece?

BAG: Yeah.

DFW: You're dividing an argumentative piece up into kind of three tragic acts, then. Because I'd resist the idea that it's dividable into three, but . . .

BAG: Do you think of most pieces as having this, in Aristotle's terms, a beginning, a middle, and an end—those three parts?

DFW: I think, like most things about writing, the answer lies on a continuum. I think the interesting question is, how much violence do you do to the piece if you reprise it in a three-act . . . a three-part structure.

BAG: Well, the middle is the biggest puzzle, I think. To say, "Oh, this is what you do in the middle." I think your statement of the opener is excellent. What about the closer? What about the end? What do *you* try to do? What are the ends in your essays?

DFW: The middle should work . . . It lays out the argument in steps, not in a robotic way, but in a way that the reader can tell (a) what the distinct steps or premises of the argument are; and (b), this is the tricky one, how they're connected to each other. So when I teach nonfiction classes, I spend a disproportionate amount of my time teaching the students how to write transitions, even as simple ones as *however* and *moreover* between sentences. Because part of their belief that the reader can somehow read their mind is their failure to see that the reader needs help understanding how two sentences are connected to each other—and also transitions between paragraphs.

I'm thinking of the argumentative things that I like the best, and because of this situation the one that pops into my mind is Orwell's "Politics and the English Language." If you look at how that's put together, there's a transition in almost every single paragraph. Right?

Like, "Moreover, not only is this offense common, but it is harmful in this way." You know where he is in the argument, but you never get the sense that he's ticking off items on a checklist; it's part of an organic whole. My guess would be, if I were an argumentative writer, that I would spend one draft on just the freaking argument, ticking it off like a checklist, and then the real writing part would be weaving it and making the transitions between the parts of the argument—and probably never abandoning the opening, never letting the reader forget what the stakes are here. Right? Never letting the reader think that I've lapsed into argument for argument's sake, but that there's always a larger, overriding purpose.

Now we've reached my horizon of ignorance. I know there's certain legal writing that's simply very formal; and it's for a judge to satisfy certain documentary requirements. And I don't think any of this stuff necessarily applies to that. I think it would probably apply much more to something like a litigator's closing statement to a jury, or something like that.

BAG: Why are transitions so important in writing?

DFW: [*pause*] Reading is a very strange thing. We get talked to about it and talk explicitly about it in first grade and second grade and third grade, and then it all devolves into interpretation. But if you think about what's going on when you read, you're processing information at an incredible rate.

One measure of how good the writing is is how little effort it requires for the reader to track what's going on. For example, I am not an absolute believer in standard punctuation at all times, but one thing that's often a big shock to my students is that punctuation isn't merely a matter of pacing or how you would read something out loud. These marks are, in fact, cues to the reader for how very quickly to organize the various phrases and clauses of the sentence so the sentence as a whole makes sense.

I believe psycholinguists, as part of neuroscience, spend . . . I mean, they hook little sensors up to readers' eyes and study this stuff. I don't know much about that, but I do know that when you're not punctuating effectively for your genre, or when you fail to supply sufficient transitions, you are upping the amount of effort the reader has to make in order . . . forget appreciate . . . simply to *understand* what it is that you are communicating. My own guess is that at just about the point where that amount—the amount of time that you're spending on a sentence, the amount of effort—becomes conscious, when you are conscious that this is hard, is the time when college students' papers begin getting marked down by the prof. Right?

But one of the things I end up saying to the students is, "Realize your professors are human beings. They're reading these things really fast, but you're often being graded down for reasons that the professor isn't consciously aware of because of an immense amount of reading and an immense amount of evaluation of the quality of a piece of writing, the qualities of the person producing it, occur below, just below, the level of consciousness, which is really the way you want it. And one of the things that really good writing does is that it's able to get across massive amounts of information and various favorable impressions of the communicator with minimal effort on the part of the reader."

That's why people use terms like *flow* or *effortless* to describe writing that they regard as really superb. They're not saying *effortless* in terms of it didn't seem like the writer spent any work. It simply requires no effort to read it—the same way listening to an incredible storyteller talk out loud requires no effort to pay attention. Whereas when you're bored, you're conscious of how much effort is required to pay attention. Does that make sense?

BAG: Yeah.

DFW: Okay.

BAG: Have you encountered . . .

DFW: That's like a seven-minute answer to a simple question.

BAG: It's great. Have you encountered people who say, "You ought to write without any explicit transitions"? Have you seen this? That you should never use . . .

DFW: Oh, that if your sentences are well wrought enough, the connection between them will be evident.

BAG: I hear this from time to time.

DFW: This is the tricky thing about talking about writing and usage. We're talking about a continuum: you overuse transitions and the writing gets labored, turgid. Or the reader feels condescended to when a connection between two thoughts that is manifest to her is some-how pounded. Right?

I mean, it's a similar thing . . . I know you've got a thing about the passive voice. The passive voice isn't always bad. If I've got a paragraph about a certain law and I say, "The law was passed in 1967," that's totally appropriate. I don't want to pull the reader's attention on the group of legislators who passed the law. But you overuse the passive voice, you're distorting the normal order of the sentences. You're filling it up, often with prepositions or with forms of the verb *to be*, which is one of the ways that writing gets flabbed out. And you're dehumaniz-ing the writing because there's no agent. Right? So it immediately becomes more abstract, so the reader's eyes glaze over quickly.

But this is what's very tricky about teaching. If you say to them, "Never use the passive voice," you're an idiot. Sometimes the passive voice is exactly what you want. But not all the time. And probably not more than 5% of sentences really need to be in the passive voice. I forget what that was an analogy with.

BAG: It's a judgment call.

DFW: Well, it's a judgment call, but it's also a feel call. One of the things that makes a really good writer is the writer can just kind of *feel* when she needs to do it, or when she needs a transition and when she doesn't. Which doesn't mean such creatures are born, but it does mean that's why practicing and paying attention never stop being important. Right? It's because we're training the same part of us that knows how to swing a golf club or shift a standard transmission, things we want to be able to do automatically. So we have to pay attention and learn how to do them so we can quit thinking about them and just do them automatically.

BAG: Why do you think so many children, not just in this country but in almost every English-speaking country, are taught not to begin sentences with conjunctions? You can't begin a sentence with *and* or *but*. My own recent findings suggest that you really can't write all that well until you're beginning 10%–20% of your sentences with conjunctions.

DFW: Really? You like it, I notice. Again, it would be a guess. Teachers have a larger agenda, which is to teach students to be able to make compound sentences with more than one independent clause. The big way to do that is with conjunctions and commas.

They're also probably trying to beat out of the students the kinds of sentences that students were exposed to when they were learning to read: "See Dick run. Period. See Jane run. Period. Dick is with Jane. Period." Right? So as part of the attempt to talk about more complicated sentences, it becomes easy to go too far and get knee-jerk and say, "Therefore, just don't do this. It's caused nothing but trouble. Don't start your sentences with *but* and *and*." When the truth is, eh, 20% of the time you're probably going to want to, but they're very special cases. So let's sit down for three hours and talk about them.

Well, you're not going to do that with a third grader. Right? That's why this is not a skill that you just learn once and you're done with it. This is . . . You're never done.

BAG: A lifelong apprenticeship?

DFW: This is a lifelong apprenticeship with aspirations to journeymanhood. Right? Yeah. But I think that's a guess. It's very easy to make fun of teachers who do this.

A teacher of mine in junior high hated me because I corrected her about *hopefully*. She said, "You never start a sentence with *hopefully*. *Hopefully* is an adverb." Right? So you never say, "Hopefully it will rain today because my crops really need it." And the truth is there's such a thing as a sentence adverb that expresses the speaker's intention, but that's college or grad-school grammar. It was appropriate in eighth grade for that teacher to tell her students, "Don't do this," because most of us were screwing up with adverbs anyway. Right?

So her nightmare was some little nerd in the back row who happened to know what a sentence adverb was. But when I look back on it, she was completely reasonable. It would have been nice if she would have said, "For now, don't do it. Later on, as part of your lifelong apprenticeship, you're going to learn there are certain adverbs that in fact are graceful at the start of a sentence. But for now, boys and girls, don't do it."

This is part of my own recovery from having hated my grammar teachers. I'm starting to realize they had reasons for what they were doing. They weren't often real smart about them, though.

BAG: What's wrong with buried verbs?

DFW: Buried verbs, which I was taught are called nominalizations, are turning a verb into a noun for kind of BS-y reasons. "I tried to facilitate the organization of the unions," instead of, "I tried to help organize the unions." People like them in bureaucratic, institutional, academic writing, I think, because some people get the idea that maximum numbers of words, maximum amount of complication, equals intelligence and erudition.

The problem with them is . . . Golly, there are a whole lot. They spawn preposition plague, they have more syllables, usually, they spawn pernicious forms of the *to be* verb, which again flabs up the writing, and very often they make the writing more abstract than it has to be.

"I tried to organize it," is a regular subject–verb–object phrase that all of us get and can understand with a minimum of effort. "I attempted to facilitate the organization of the unions," simply requires more work. It's stupid.

Let me stop you. I don't remember your entry on buried verbs. Is that what's wrong?

BAG: Yeah, I think they're unduly abstract.

DFW: But sometimes, obviously, if you're refer-
ring to *litigation*, you've got to use the
buried verb.

BAG: Right, you can't always say *litigate*.

DFW: Then there's always the—what do you
call it?—buried nouns, like, "We need
to dialogue about this," "You gifted me
with this," which make my stomach
hurt even more than the buried verbs. I
guess those, a lot of those are more vogue
words.

BAG: Linguists call it functional shift, where
you press a noun into service as a verb.
Some kinds of functional shift are not so
bothersome—using a noun as an adjec-
tive, "We've got a room problem here,"
you know, that kind of thing.

DFW: But you're right, yeah, the noun-to-verb
thing is more annoying in a vogue-word
sense. But you're right. Buried verbs are a

quick way to turn a clean, elegant, simple clause into a clotted nightmare.

BAG: Yep. Why is verbosity a bad thing?

DFW: Isn't *verbosity*, the term itself, pejorative? Is this not a loaded question? *Verbose* is not neutral.

BAG: Why is it bad to have extra words in a sentence?

DFW: Doesn't *extra*, itself, imply . . . It's very . . . I don't think verbosity, in terms of using a lot of words, is always a bad thing artistically. In the kind of writing that we're talking about, there are probably two big dangers. One is that it makes the reader work harder, and that's never good. The other is that if the reader becomes conscious that she's having to work harder because you're being verbose, now she's apt not only to dislike the piece of writing; she's apt to draw certain conclusions about you as a person that are unfavorable. So you run the risk of losing kind of both your logical appeal and your ethical appeal.

Now, this is presuming that you've got a reader who is bright, literate, well-educated, and paying attention. Given the amount of verbosity—particularly in bureaucratic, institutional, legal, and scientific writing, including the stuff that gets published—indicates to me that there are certain audiences that aren't especially bothered by this. Why that is I don't know except that a lot of them tend to be audiences composed of professionals who went through a long apprenticeship that meant reading huge amounts of this kind of stuff, and they sort of got brainwashed or maybe inured to it in some way. From the point of view, like you, of somebody who just loves the language and thinks it's hard enough to be clear anyway, in the default case the fewest words, each of which is the small-est and plainest possible, is usually the best policy.

You need
to quack
this way.

BAG: Why are bureaucrats prone to officialese?

DFW: Do you explain in your seminar what you mean by *officialese*?

BAG: Um . . .

DFW: I've got a pretty good idea of what you mean.

BAG: Official-sounding words. You hear at LAX, for example, "Please maintain visual contact with your personal property at all times." That's a kind of amalgamation of different kinds of officialese. You hear it in hotels: "How may I be of assistance." "Do you require one evening or two?"

DFW: Yep.

BAG: You hear it, "Prior to your departure."

DFW: Yep. Tell you what. I'll give what I think is the true answer. If it's too long or wandering, ask it again and we can do it quicker.

BAG: Okay.

DFW: One answer is the fact that people, unless they're paying attention, tend to confuse fanciness with intelligence or authority. For me, I've noodled about this a fair amount because a lot of this sort of language afflicts me. My guess is this: officialese, as spoken by officials, is meant to empty the communication of a certain level of humanity. On purpose.

If I'm delivering a press release as an official, I'm speaking not as David

Wallace. I'm speaking as the deputy assistant commissioner in charge of whatever. I'm speaking with and for some sort of bureaucratic entity. My guess is one of the reasons why we as a people tolerate, or even expect, this officialese is that we associate it with a different form of communication than interpersonal—Dave and Bryan talking together. That the people who are speaking are in many senses speaking not as human beings but as the larynx and tongue of a larger set of people, responsibilities, laws, regulations, whatever. And that is probably why, even though it's dreadfully ugly to the ear and why if you think hard about it, "Keep your personal belongings in visual contact at all times" is actually likely to be understood by a smaller percentage of people than, "Please keep an eye on your stuff at all times."

Nevertheless, there are imperatives behind using the language that way. And some of it is to be antihuman.

BAG: What do you suppose would happen
to an American airline, not necessarily
American Airlines, but all the airlines
use officialese . . . What do you suppose
would happen to that airline if you and
I were hired to rewrite all their spiels in
good, plain, humane English? Would
that be a business drag on that company,
or would it be good for them?

DFW: I think the really interesting question
is why hasn't this been done before?
It would be a fascinating experiment.
Here's my guess. It would be a great mar-
keting device. It would be a way to look
different from other airlines. It would
sound more human. Right? I mean, we
always get these corporations: "We care
about you. Therefore, we proactively
try to facilitate your growing business
needs." Well, that second clause com-
municates the opposite of "We care about
you" because that second clause isn't
a human-to-human contact. My guess
is, initially it would be really good, but
then maybe you'd find stuff like it was
harder to keep passengers in line, it was

more difficult to placate them when there were flight delays because they now felt a human connection to the airline, and were less apt, maybe, to docilely go sit, but were more apt to bitch the airline out the way you'd bitch a friend out.

I don't know. I've stopped thinking, "Gosh darn it, I wish they would just simply start speaking good English," and started thinking that . . . You know what? There are reasons behind this stuff. Very complicated reasons. I'm not sure they're good reasons or not, but there are reasons. And we really don't know what the consequences would be if we all started using English in human, urgent, interpersonal tones in all kinds of public situations.

BAG: Sometimes it verges on doublespeak. For example, the signs in American Airlines' gates say, "Beverages only in main cabin." Now, as somebody who travels a lot and gets upgraded, I first thought . . .

DFW: "Those poor thirsty first-class passengers."

BAG: Yeah! "I'm in first class, I'm going to want a beverage as well." Well in fact what it means is you don't get a meal if you're in coach, but they say, "Beverages only in main cabin."

DFW: But see, that's not just an example of officialese, that's just, that's just somebody who's being hamhanded with the language. That person hasn't been taught that where you stick *only* in a sentence completely changes [the meaning], right? "I only love you" versus "I love only you." Yeah, it's fun to make fun of that stuff. I've started thinking . . . There's a lot of advertising stuff that's really ridiculous. Right? There's *special, super special,* [*raising voice*] *mega super special,* triple exclamation points!!! Or my favorite as a child was "Save up to 50% *and more*." "Save up to 50% and more." Mom and I would laugh about this.

It's occurred to me, though, that it's possible that advertising English is a dialect unto itself—very different from regular English. And its main job is to penetrate your consciousness. They figure you're not paying much attention, you're numbed, you're overwhelmed with advertising, so they don't care whether it's right or not, whether it makes sense, they just want in. So they shout at you. It may be that *up to and more* has been shown statistically to increase your ability to memorize the 50%. The point is not that this is okay. I think it's damaging to the language as a beautiful thing, and to interhuman communication, but I've stopped thinking that it's just idiots who weren't paying attention in eighth grade and don't know how to do this stuff.

In fact, I think there are probably about a thousand different professional dialects of English, and they're often motivated by incredibly complicated premises, maybe about half of which are conscious and developed by high-paid specialists and surveyors and stuff, and the other half involve this groupthink, group hypnosis, the same stuff that lies behind academese or jargon or any of that kind of stuff.

You want to spend a fun couple of years sometime? I'd love to see *Garner's Dictionary of Dialectal English Usage*. And I don't just mean neo-Gaelic West Virginia. I mean advertising English, bureau-cratic English, corporate English, hipster English . . . because I will bet that just trying to figure out some of the codes and motives behind them would just be fascinating. It would be hard for you because you love standard English and all of this other stuff seems like a debase-ment of it—as I think it is, too. But it's not a debasement the way somebody who's just blundering around having no idea what they're doing is debasing.

BAG: Which is almost preferable debasement.

DFW: Well, you get down to certain axioms about what the language is and what it ought to be used for. And you and I, I think, are essentially gooey-hearted humanists, and we want it to vivify and facilitate . . . we want it to help inter-human relationships of various sorts.

But language is also a tool of persuasion. Propaganda, right? We have a president who apparently doesn't need to use the language well because as he's speaking, behind us are little banners—talk about Orwellian—"Fighting the War on Terrorism." Right? Have you seen this? These press conferences? No longer do we need a president who's an example of an articulate, thoughtful person because we've got behind him this sort of almost hypnotic set of messages that someone has discovered that, with some base, those actually work better at creating a favorable impression than having a well-spoken, apparently thoughtful president.

I don't mean to bust on the president, I'm just saying that in today's business and political climate when you've got such specialization, you've got people who are so good at seeking to get what they want, whether those are votes or acquiescence or consumer behavior, there are uses of language that to you and me are horrible and a debasement, but are completely deliberate and, within the rules of that discipline, possibly effective, including "Save up to 50% or more."

BAG: Don't you think if President George W. Bush softened his dialect a bit, he could still speak as a Texan speaks? But if he were able—and he may not be able—to soften the dialect a bit, he could actually mitigate the credibility problem that he has with so many people all over the country.

DFW: Well . . . [*pause*] I don't know about that. What interests me about Bush linguistically is he seems to me to be walking a very thin wire . . . Well, he's not walking a wire. What's the term? He's torn in two different directions. And I'm sure he's got people around him who are . . .

On the one hand, his political viability is partly a matter of his being seen as like a man of the people. On the other hand, he's our number-one bureaucrat and is required to speak officialese. And I don't think . . . Even if you assume he's good at certain stuff, it's clear there's some kind of missing sulcus, or even possible organic damage in his brain when it comes to being able to form complicated sentences, especially when they are, like, abstract nouns or weird conditional tenses that he's just not very, very good at it. Somewhere, someone has made the decision that having him spew all these malapropisms, though it opens him up to ridicule to a certain percentage of well-educated people—who are probably not the people who are going to vote for him anyway—somehow has a positive effect for people in his base.

Why that is I don't know. I'm not privy to the theory, I'm not privy to the census data. But there are too many highly paid political pros around him for someone not to have suggested the idea that he become, you know, that he move closer to Will Rogers on the continuum and stop trying to use this officialese that he's even worse than his father at. Right? I mean, in a way, it's delicious because he so mangles it that it shows up officialese for what ugly BS it really is, but someone somewhere has decided that it is in his political and governmental interest to do this. And it's fascinating.

BAG: Have you noticed how when he reads a speech he sounds almost like a third grader, saying /thee/ every time and /ay/, /thee **nay**-shun/ and /ay **nay**-shun/, but not /uh **nay**-shun/ or /thuh **nay**-shun/ the way almost any other American would?

DFW: Yep. Part of what I know about him I know from the Lemann article in *The New Yorker*,* but he is apparently interpersonally, one on one, amazing—a Mozart.

---

* Nicholas Lemann, "Remember the Alamo: How George W. Bush Reinvented Himself." *New Yorker*, October 18, 2004, 148–61.

He's just very, very bad at public pre-
sentations of language. And I can only
imagine what it must cost him to do it
over and over and over and over again.
I don't have much sympathy for the guy
politically, but you talk about somebody
who's looked, from early on in the first
campaign, just out of his element linguistically, communicatively . . .

What's fascinating and really scary
is that this appears not to matter—or
even to be a plus. Right? And it's not
that Carter with his *nucular*, or Bill
Clinton had his share of solecisms, too,
but, we're so far now from a Kennedy
or a Woodrow Wilson or an FDR that it
becomes tempting to think that our own
instincts for what language use means
about the person, not just about the
person's intelligence, but their character,
their forthrightness, are just . . . everything's different now.

And people like you and me, we
just don't have our finger on the pulse
anymore. What people are looking for
is not the kind of stuff we're talking

about. You'll want to cut this out. I don't say that to my students because my line with them is still, "Look, you're at this elite school, you're going to end up in the professions . . . Right? You need to quack this way." Forget all this stuff about it being beautiful and having centuries of tradition and being the adventure of a lifetime. But the truth is that between sophisticated advertising and national-level politics, I am at a loss as to what people's use of language is now meant to convey and connote to the receiver. It's so different from the way I myself am wired that I just don't get it. I'm looking forward to starting to read stuff about it because somebody's going to notice this.

BAG: We have a lot of different cultures in our one culture. If we have a culture.

DFW: Yeah.

BAG: Well . . .

DFW: But we also have a mass culture. And the two things that I'm talking about—advertising and national politics—are occurring at kind of the mass level.

BAG: Yeah.

DFW: I'm not talking about the purity. I'm not some Gaullist, you know: "The purity of English is being violated by all these . . ." It's not that. It's that "Save up to 50% and more" is, in a certain dialect, worth millions of dollars—probably a better thing to say than "Save up to 50%." That's funky if you think about it. And literally Orwellian.

BAG: Let me ask you this. If plain language is a good thing, why is it also a good thing to have an ample vocabulary?

DFW: Well, for a couple of reasons.

One, plain language doesn't mean all little, monosyllabic words. The general rule of thumb is you use the very smallest word that will do in a particular situation. Sometimes the situation you're describing is specific and technical, and a small word won't do.

Probably the other big thing is that there's this thing called "elegant variation." You have to be able . . . In order for your sentences not to make the reader's eyes glaze over, you can't simply use the same core set of words, particularly important nouns and verbs, over and over and over again. You have to have synonyms at your fingertips and alternative constructions at your fingertips. And usually, though not in the sense of memorizing vocab words like we were kids, but having a larger vocabulary is usually the best way to do that. The best. Having a good vocabulary ups the chances that we're going to be able to know the right word, even if that's the plainest word that will do and to achieve some kind of elegant variation, which I am kind of a fiend for.

BAG: You like elegant variation?

DFW: Well, it just drives me crazy. You have . . . You probably won't cover it, but I know you have a little tweaky question in here, like "Do you like acronyms or not?" Right?

BAG: What *do* you think of acronyms?

DFW: That was the question. Let me explain to the camera. There's a fair amount of my stuff that has a lot of acronyms in it. Actually, technically I think they're initialisms because I don't usually make them into words.

BAG: *Snoot* is an acronym.

DFW: *Snoot* is an acronym, but I often like to abbreviate. This happened in a math book I wrote where, you know, the Bolzano–Weierstrass Theorem would get alternated with BWT, which was probably . . . Sometimes you can get away with it, if the reader's got the original thing locked into mind. I err too far on the side of using too many of these things because I hate saying *Bolzano–Weierstrass Theorem* over and over and over and over again. And I start getting this thing where I want to be very high-level and very offhand. But I get some of the energy behind the question, and it's one of my problems. I need to chill on it a little bit.

BAG: I've got to know the answer to this: What is your theory of capitalizing, especially in "Authority and American Usage"? And is that typical of your writing generally?

DFW: That was a mess. There were certain big, abstract terms—*democracy, authority*—that I wanted to capitalize in that. But the problem, then . . . I urge your watchers, your seminar attendees, to abjure this habit because then . . . The problem with that essay, and believe me, the copy editor when the book version came out, the copy editor, my ears were burning because she was so annoyed by this. Say

I want to use the word *authority* in a capital-letter sense, but now it appears several other times before I explain the cap versus lowercase sense, so do I cap it or not? And it ends up being a nightmare. That essay represented for me the nadir of my experience with trying to juggle caps, LCs, ital, and stuff in quotations, like tone quotes. It just became a nightmare. I apologize. I meant no offense to you, but it ended up just being a ghastly mess.

BAG: Were you happier with the full-length version that appeared in *Consider the Lobster* than you were with the one that appeared as "Tense Present" in *Harper's*?

DFW: Well, sure. *Harper's* cuts real well. This is part of the problem with what I do: I end up giving them five times as much as they can use sometimes. With the *Harper's* piece, it was maybe twice as much. Which means I need magazines that cut real well, or editors who cut real well. *Harper's*, they cut it okay, but they cut out most of the things that for them were dry or academic, which was actually the meat. They left in, like, pants analogies that were funny and zingy, but the actual essay is meant to advance a certain kind of argument through both fairly meticulous—not scholarly because it's more pop than that—and fairly sedulous argumentation, and zingy, pop, informal things, and they cut out a lot of the sedulous stuff. The *Harper's* article is probably more fun to read. The version that's in the book, I think, is a heck of a lot better, *pace* the terrible capitalization and ital versus [*rolling eyes*] tone-quote question.

BAG: *The Guardian* . . . Do you read the reviews?

DFW: No, no, only because they make me insane. Even if it's a nice review, I'll focus only on the one or two bad reviews.

BAG: You don't want me to even tell you?

DFW: Oh, you can, no, it's fine.

BAG: Well, *The Guardian* said that the usage essay was worth the entire price of the book.

DFW: Really?

BAG: Yes. *The Independent* said it was the worst thing in the book.

DFW: Yeah, yeah.

BAG: You know, it's interesting.

DFW: Yeah, yeah. If you're somewhat interested in this stuff, this stuff is fascinating. If you're not . . . Right? I mean what are the two subjects . . .

BAG: But how could somebody not be?

DFW: Grammar, algebra. You . . . this kind of stuff to some people . . . I'm only just getting to be able to reach students who, literally, their nictitating membrane comes down when you start mentioning this stuff abstractly. And things like date analogies or why you dress a certain way for job interviews are just my hamhanded way to try to put this in a kind of tableau that's got some voltage for them. That makes this a metaphor. To try to put it in some way that they can feel something about. You recognize this, right? You're at a party: "Yo, what's your hobby?" "Usage." "Huh, huh, huh! Boy, I bet you get laid a lot!"

BAG: Yeah, right.

DFW: I mean it's . . . you know. But I can introduce you to some ladies in Manhattan where you'd be like Mick Jagger. Right? It's a very weird thing. It's also a very elitist thing. People who care about this tend to be super well-educated, super-high SAT scores, they're often in the professions. I mean, not always, but . . . So it gets politically charged. Are we, have we . . . ?

BAG: Yeah, I want to ask you one last question. I've taken you way over. What's wrong with genteelisms like *prior to* and *subsequent to*?

DFW: Well, I have trouble parsing your question. *Genteelism* seems to me to be an overly charitable way to characterize them. To me, they're puff words, like using *utilize* instead of *use*. Which in 99 cases out of 100 is just stupid. Or *individual* for *person*, more syllables, it's just puffed up.

Why say *prior to* rather than *before*? Everybody knows what *before* means, it's fewer words. And I think technically, given the Latin roots, it should be *posterior to* if you're going to use *prior to*. So if you're saying *prior to* and *subsequent to*, you're in fact, in a very high-level way, messing up grammatically. But would you ever want to say *posterior to*? No. So you don't say *prior to*.

But you'll notice, this is the downside of starting to pay attention. You start noticing all of the people who say *at this time* rather than *now*. Why did they just take up one third of a second of my lifetime making me parse *at this time*, rather than just saying *now* to me? And you start being bugged.

But you get to be more careful and attentive in your own writing, so you become an agent of light and goodness rather than the evil that's all around us.

BAG: But the weird thing is that almost every American today does say *prior to*. And this is a commonplace puffed-up thing, I think it's partly why I call it a genteelism.

DFW: And it is probably approaching that fabled thing, "The Garner Skunked Term." If it becomes the default usage for a certain percentage of . . . Look, the only reason not to use it, rhetorically, is it's going to bug snoots, right? At a certain point, snoots will stop being bugged.

But it's also true that, to a large extent, our linguistic lives aren't fully conscious. Right? It's too much. It's too fast. I believe it is better to pay attention and to try to make your language as beautiful and graceful and adroit as possible. But a whole lot of people couldn't care less and are reinforced in that by having traumatic, boring, upsetting experiences in school around grammar and stuff. So a lot of people just aren't paying very close attention.

BAG: And the people who couldn't care less are likely to say they *could* care less.

DFW: Oh, that's right. So I made the reverse error. I said, "Couldn't care less," as if it were an error. Yeah, yeah. . . . Although Steven Pinker has that whole phonetic, sonic representation of *I could care less* that's supposed to explain why. It makes no sense! [*throws up hands*] Even the spiky thing doesn't make sense. It's not . . . Anyway, we'll talk about Pinker on some other tape.

BAG: Well, David Foster Wallace, thank you very much for coming by.

DFW: Bryan Garner, you're very welcome. You guys are in good hands; you trust this man right here. [*Drumming thighs and preparing to stand*]

Index

a & the, pronunciation of, 109–10
ABCs of Handwriting Analysis, The (Santoy), 16n
abstractness, 43–45
abstruse vs. *obtuse*, 69
acronyms and initialisms, 114–15
advertising English, 104–05
airlinese, 101–02
algebra, 118
Allen, J.P., 16
American Airlines, 101, 103
American Law Institute, 3
Amherst College, 32–33
and, beginning sentences with, 90–92
apprenticeship as writer and reader, 92, 93, 97
argumentative writing, 77–90
Aristotle, 82
articles, pronunciation of, 109–10
at this time vs. *now*, 120–21
"Authority and American Usage" (a.k.a. "Tense Present") (Wallace), 1–2, 13–15, 25, 67, 115–18

bathroom reading, 72–73
Biaggi's, 7
Black's Law Dictionary (Garner, ed.), 4
Blood Meridian (McCarthy), 60
Bolzano–Weierstrass Theorem, 115
book reviews, 78–79

Bunker, M.N., 16n
bureaucrats, 98–105
buried verbs, 93–96
Bush, George W., 45, 106–10
but, beginning sentences with, 90–92

capitalization, 115–16, 117
Carter, Jimmy, 110
census, 69
Claremont Colleges, 9, 12, 14, 40
clarity, 44–45
clichés, 56
Clinton, Bill, 110
college writing teachers, 46–49
communicative vs. expressive writing, 33–35
conjunctions as sentence-starters, 90–92
Connection, The, 4
consensus, 69
Consider the Lobster (Wallace), 2, 15, 17, 116–17
corporate English, 98–105
correspondence, 1–2, 9–10, 13–14, 67
couldn't care less vs. *could care less*, 122
crossing out name, 15–18
culture, 110–12

dating, 38
death, 63
Delillo, Don, 9, 74
d'Gabriel, Treyce, 16n

Dictionary of Modern American Usage, A (Garner), 1, 3, 74
drafts, 30–31, 65–66, 70
drug use, 32

editing, proofreading, and revision, 70
effects of politics on language, 111–12
elegant variation, 113–14
e-mails, 55–56
endings, 82–83
English, shifting direction of, 110–112
Entourage, 15
Erdrich, Louise, 60
exercises for effective writing, 27, 28–29, 36–37
expressive vs. communicative writing, 33–35

fewer vs. *less*, 52
fiction workshops, 36–38
first drafts, 65
Forster, E.M., 18
Four Seasons (Georgetown), 13
Freeman, Brian, 11
Frolic of His Own, A (Gaddis), 74–75
functional shift, 95

Gaddis, William, 74
Garner, Caroline, 13
Garner's Dictionary of Dialectal English Usage, 106
Garner's Dictionary of Legal Usage, 73–74

Garner's Modern American Usage, 1, 3, 74
Gass, William, 9
Gaullism, 112
genteelisms, 120–21
Good Will Hunting, 40
Google Images, 18
grammar, 31–32, 118
Green, Karen (DFW's wife), 12, 50–52, 61
Guardian, The, 117–18

Hand, Learned, 74
handwriting analysis, 15–18
Handwriting Analysis (Bunker), 16n
Harper's, 2, 3, 13, 116–17
Harry Ransom Center, 19
Harvard Co-Op, 3–4
Hilton Checkers Hotel, 7, 11, 21
hipster English, 105
hopefully, 92–93
Hunting, Will, 40
hypercorrection, 54–55

I vs. *me*, 54–55
Independent, The, 118
Infinite Jest (Wallace), 1
initialisms and acronyms, 114–15
Internal Revenue Code, 48
interviews with judges and justices, 11, 13–14

Jagger, Mick, 119
jargon, 34, 43–45, 47–49
Jones, James, 29
judges as readers, 44–45

Kennedy, John F., 110
Kilpatrick, James J., 11
King James Version, 60

language as tool of persuasion, 106
lawyers, 5, 43, 63, 66, 68, 73, 74–75
LAX, 98–99
Learning to Write (Stevenson), 28
legal writing, 84
legal-writing seminars, 5–6, 8
Lemann, Nicholas, 11, 109
less vs. *fewer*, 52
letters, 55–56
Lewis, Anthony, 3–4
Lincoln, Abraham, 20
literary criticism, 43–45
literary papers as arguments, 79
longhand vs. typing, 29–30

Maine Lobster Festival, 5
marriage, 11–12
McCarthy, Cormac, 60
McCormick & Schmick's, 11
me vs. *I*, 54–55

memos, 55–56
middles, 81–85
mind-reading, 26–27, 77–78

nation, 109
New Fowler's Modern English Usage, The
 (Burchfield), 70, 72
New Republic, The, 2, 67
New Yorker, The, 109
New York Review of Books, The, 2
New York Times, The, 3
nominalizations, 93–96
nonfiction, 57–58, 60, 65–66, 68, 76–78, 83
now vs. *at this time*, 120–21
nuclear, 110

obtuse vs. *abstruse*, 69
"O Captain! My Captain!" (Whitman), 20–21
officialese, 98–105, 108, 110
only, 69, 103
Only Handwriting Book You Will Ever Need, The
 (d'Gabriel), 16n
openers, 80–81
organizing research, 65–66, 76–79
Orwell, George, 83–84, 106, 112
outlining, 76–79
overcomplication, 43–45, 47–49
Oxford English Dictionary (OED), 71, 72
Ozick, Cynthia, 60

passive voice, 89–90
Pinker, Steven, 122
plain language, 97, 101–02, 112–13
Poe, Edgar Allan, 57–58
"Politics and the English Language" (Orwell),
    83–84
Pomona College, 9, 12, 40
postcards, 10
posterior to, 120
postscript, 10
precision, 44–45
preparing to write, 65–66, 76–78
prior to, 120–21
professional dialects, 104–05
professors as writers and readers, 44, 46–49,
    86–87
pronouns, 54–55
propaganda, 106–07
psycholinguists, 86
public radio, 4
punctuation, 85

readers, 34–35, 44–46, 86–87, 96–97
"Remember the Alamo" (Lemann), 109
research, 65–66
rewriting, 30–31
Rogers, Will, 109
Roget's Thesaurus, 71, 72
Roosevelt, Franklin Delano, 110
Rosen, Billie Pesin, 16n

Roy E. Disney Professorship, 9
Russell, Bertrand, 56

Safire, William, 9
Santoy, Claude, 16n
save up to 51% and more, 103–04, 107
Scalia, Antonin, 13–15
Scalia, Christopher, 13, 14
Science of Handwriting Analysis, The (Rosen), 16n
signing books, 15–18
Simon, John, 11
skunked terms, 121–22
slang, 53–54
snoot, 12, 114–15
snuff-dipping, 8–9
social climbing, 53–55
SoRelle, Andrea, 1
State Farm Insurance Company, 5, 9
stationery, 10
Stevenson, Robert Louis, 28
style, mimicking, 43–46
subsequent to, 120

teaching, 32–33, 34, 41–42, 69–70
teenage slang, 53–55
"Tense Present" (a.k.a. "Authority and American Usage") (Wallace), 1–2, 13–15, 25, 67, 115–18
the & *a*, pronunciation of, 109–10
thesaurus, 69, 71

This Is Water (Wallace), 18–19
transitions, 83–90
Trimble, John, 9–10
Turow, Scott, 75
typing vs. longhand, 29–30

Updike, John, 56
usage dictionaries, 68–74

verbosity, 43–45, 47–49, 96–98
vocabulary, 112–13
vogue words, 49–53, 95

Wallace, David Foster,
    admired writers, 59–61
    autograph style, 15–18
    beautiful, graceful, adroit language, 121–22
    "crummy, turgid, verbose, abstruse, abstract,
        solecism-ridden prose," 47–48
    cycles in a writer's work, 63–65
    dinners with Garner, 5, 6–9
    essential books for writers, 69
    experiences in school, 27–31
    first meeting with Garner, 6
    Garner interview on language arranged and
        conducted, 9–10
    growing up in a culture of reading, 31–32
    humor, 6, 9

joint interview with Garner on public radio, 4

joy of reading and writing, 61–62

parents, 6, 7, 8–9, 28

poetic e-mail address, 20

"quack this way," 111

"reader cannot read your mind," 26–27

self-assessment as writer, 56–59

suicide, 18

tobacco, 8–9, 10–11

"trunk cable into the linguistic heart," 73

Wallace, James, 6, 8–9

Wallace, Sally Foster, 6, 7, 8–9, 31–32

WBUR, 4

Webster's Dictionary, 68

White, Richard Grant, 9

Whitman, Walt, 20–21

Wilson, Woodrow, 110

wordiness, 43–45, 47–49, 96–98

workshops for writers, 36–38

writing,

argumentative writing, 77–90

as art, 40–42

communicative vs. expressive, 33–35

doing it well, 25–29, 55–59

drafts, 30–31, 65–66, 70

endings, 82–83

for peers, 47–49

learning to write well, 25–27

longhand, 29–30

middles, 81–85
nonfiction, 57–58, 60, 65, 66, 68, 76–78, 83
openers, 80–81
outlines, 77–79
preparation, 65–66, 76–78
spirit over intellect, 35
transitions, 83–84, 85–86, 88–89, 90
verbosity, 43–45, 47–49, 95–98
writing skills as bridge to other communication
skills, 41–42

It was an accidental friendship if ever there was one. David Foster Wallace was at the center of late-20th-century American literature, Bryan A. Garner at that of legal scholarship and lexicography. It was language that drew them together, and it was DFW who reached out to BAG. It was DFW who penned "Authority and American Usage," the encomium to Garner's dictionary of American usage. The 95-page essay appeared first in *Harper's* in abridged form and in its full-length version in *Consider the Lobster*. It was an auspicious beginning for their friendship.

The interview reproduced here memorializes 67 minutes of their second and final evening together, in February 2006. It was DFW's last long interview, and the only one of its kind in subject matter. Would it were not so.

Royalties from this volume support the Wallace literary archive housed in the Harry Ransom Center, the University of Texas at Austin.

Colophon

The introduction and interview pages are set in 12-point Book Antiqua, a Microsoft font originally designed by Monotype in imitation of Hermann Zapf's Palatino. The face here is slightly bolder than Palatino and has distinctive italic glyphs. The accent typeface is Corbel, designed by Jeremy Tankard for Microsoft in 2005. Pages were laid out by Jeff Newman at LawProse, Inc. in Dallas. The cover was designed by Bryan and Karolyne Garner.